ADVANCE·PRAIS

Ablation is stunning in its inventiveness and shape, the touchability of both text and image combine to form a strikingly rich book. It was exhilarating to spend time with.

—Hanif Abdurraqib, author of *A Little Devil in America* (Random House, 2021)

In *Ablation*, Danika Stegeman finds a form, a 'grief box' to contain all the wounds and repairs we live and die through, their delicate debris—the torn and cut edges, pins and needles, buttons and string. This is a quiet yet viscerally felt book about pain and personal history, the 'relentless' work of time. 'If I'm / haunted,' she writes, 'then I'm / loved.'"

—Elisa Gabbert, author of *Normal Distance* (Soft Skull Press, 2022)

I am reminded in reading Danika Stegeman's *Ablation* of another complex work of hybridity, Roland Barthes' *Camera Lucida,* which like *Ablation* has at its center the loss of a mother. Both writers use grief as a kind of lens to distort and focus, to clarify and recast, to theorize, trouble, and lament. But *here* is the work of a poet and not a philosopher, and we find a dense, beautiful lyricism carrying us forward, at once poignant, elaborate, and inventive, at once fragmented and whole. As in her first book, *Pilot,* this very contemporary verse brings to us anew ancient pleasures that are and have been *poetry.*

—Eric Pankey author of *Not Yet Transfigured* (Orison Books, 2021)

Danika Stegeman's *Ablation* is a (w)reckoning. I read it outside on a humid summer day in one sitting. The sky looked like rain. At times, I had to pause and close the book—some of the material is intense—intensely painful, vividly articulated—and yet, I couldn't stop wanting to be in the air of these poems, in the art(fullness) of these poems, with the speaker of these poems. Near the end of the book, I suddenly felt raindrops, but then I realized it wasn't raining—I was actually crying. Lyrical, ecstatic, and fearless, *Ablation* is soaked in personal history, family trauma, and a formal dexterity that few poets writing today are brave enough to apply—especially in contexts (like this one) where they have something clear that they want to say/express. This is a masterful and incandescent sequence of poems—a book I will not forget and one I will recommend "to stop the world fluttering" and remind us of the power of Poetry.

—Matt Hart author of *Familiar* (Pickpocket Books, 2022)

In *Ablation*, Danika Stegeman builds vessels for her grief that open and close like night flowers. In the visible and invisible world of the mathematics of living and dying, Stegeman offers equations of isolation and invention, "If I'm / haunted then I'm / loved," and oblique architectures, "I paper / a world from slits / and folds. Glaciers are a forceful motif throughout, in their inexorable and impersonal advance, in their coldness and distance, and their epic, mostly submerged mirroring of life in motion. This book is "a hologram redoubling" bound with slippages, unfoldings, and, especially, through its aching attentiveness, a primal, burning love.

—Sun Yung Shin author of *The Wet Hex* (Coffee House Press, 2022)

Ablation plunges the reader into the messy, aching, multifarious fact of a severed-and-not mother-daughter relationship. Defined by captivating and unnerving symmetries, each poem is a shattered window meticulously taped into a mandala. Scarred light pours through. What can I say? Stegeman has written this generation's great elegy.

—Joe Hall author of *Fugue and Strike* (Black Ocean, 2023)

If I'm / haunted, then I'm / loved…" writes Danika Stegeman in her breathtaking second collection, *Ablation*. This book laments the loss and honors the memory of complicated love. But no, I wrote that wrong: love is not complicated, people are. This book is voiced and populated by people—mothers, siblings, sports stars—doing their imperfect best for one another on a planet we continually fail. Haven't we all tried "desperately to protect the people [we] loved, with what magic, dark or light, [we] could muster"? Throughout these poems, form, fragment, and ephemera elucidate the glacial grief and joy of that work.

—Paula Cisewski author of *Quitter* (Diode Editions, 2016)

Grief weaves a complicated web in Danika Stegeman's *Ablation*. While a spider works with threads of silk, Stegeman—with an equal deftness—entwines language into a complex and glimmering network. When any strand is touched, a reverberation is felt throughout the whole. "Trauma / passes across / generations. / This is / what's meant by circulatory / system," writes Stegeman, binding the physical, psychological, and emotional: body, mind, and heart. And it is a heart—that fist-sized muscle driving blood, that fist-sized muscle linked to love—pulsing at the core of Stegeman's collection. *Ablation* is a quiet, powerfully resonant book, using hybrid elements to demonstrate the overlapping immediacy of life and loss with the bizarreness of the grief that is born from the death of a parent. Guided by Stegeman's skilled hands, readers of *Ablation* will navigate the knotted pathways of shared familial history to emerge thrumming with sorrow and celebration of life.

—Jenny Irish, author of *Lupine* (Black Lawrence Press, 2023)

ABLATION

Danika Stegeman

Requests for permission should be directed to 1111@1111press.com, or mailed to 11:11 Press LLC, 11:11 Press, P.O. Box #11, Dundas, MN, 55019

Design by Mike Corrao

Paperback: 9781948687652

Printed in the United States of America

FIRST AMERICAN EDITION

9 8 7 6 5 4 3 2

For my mom

and for Vera
may all your days be gold my child

I mouth the word
"motherless,"

and it's a cut that misses, a cut made clean, the clasp of a
snapdragon's jaw. I mouth the words *corn hopper, hair combs,*
hand-painted flowers, grayscale photos with Exacto knife edges.
I keep these things in a box.

Anxiety pins me in place. I've got 60 needles aimed at my center,
one point for each year of her life. I stare at cracks in the asphalt
and can't seem to leave the parking lot. The funeral home's across a street
torn to gravel they'll repave next week. I move forward to hug my friend,
but he and his wife move away slightly. My mom has died during a pandemic.
The air's not safe. Don't touch your face. For God's sake,

                                          don't touch each other
                                          or speak closely.

I feel like a thousand dead birds, one brother says. It'll take months
to transfuse our veins with sand and several more before we can bear
the heat of our blood again.

I tried to watch the sunset, but I couldn't, the other brother says, *the clouds
got in the way*. It's overcast but refuses to rain until we've left for the quiet
of our homes.

Weeks later, the sky's heart still bends light, but it matters less. Handful of red, handful of copper. My sister speaks in tongues, but what she's asking for is money. Her loss sharpens. She tucks cash in her pockets and places the sympathy cards in front of me. I face the stack and cut the leaves out, then add them to my grief box. I mishear her words as *dust in my heart, wind in my hair.*

I don't need anything.

The sun bleeds through the clouds. I look up,
and cut paper leaves pour from my eyes.

Ablation

My mom,
as a dark-haired
girl, lay still to keep her
heart from fluttering. A glacier
lapses
time, moves
through variations and exists
as many glaciers, a
palimpsest shorn
present.

See through
the window panes
of my eyes. Same/not-same
chromosomes mutate a me into a
you. Love
like a radar map. Love like
infrared. Love like heat
or light pouring
in waves.

I want
to show you how
my life feels. I've given
you my life. Cumulus clouds move
in a
wall. Heat
lightning. I wash my face in a
basin of rain, count the
molecules in
prisms.

All my
life might fit in
my mom's right atrium,
in her tachycardic, too-fast
heart. I
fear I
carry incoherence in my
genes. Glaciers recede. Holes
open where walls
should be.

This is
home, a planet
of trees. Ablation means
the surgical removal of
body
tissue;
or, the evaporation of
a glacier. My ice-scraped
land. My cover
of snow.

As you're
born I become
liminal; line as ice
is a line. I count seconds like
platelets.
Our hearts
beat a finite number. We're not
inexhaustible, drawn
between water
and air.

When I
say you, I mean
daughter. I mean reader.
I mean for you to rest in the
hollow
my heart
shapes and unshapes. The morning fog's
half in, half out. The leaves drift
in part-circles,
undone.

My mom as dark-
haired girl. Little ghost-
body lying still to
stop the world fluttering.

CARD

This space for Address Only

A note
resounds, birdsong
you sing back to the bird.
Transmogrified, I molt into
some new
figure,
this mother, this loosening knot.
The bird's wings spread, meadow-
blown beneath a
day moon.

River-
stained dress worn thread-
bare, or, how to become
the climate by absorbing it.
We peer
through rust-
written doors: *your cells contain the
universe.* Aquatic
ecosystems
in jars.

The page
constitutes a
present and stakes a frame
that you'll outbrave. I fall asleep
to the
sound your
heart makes. Like plaster lining walls
into rooms, I paper
a world from slits
and folds.

Treefall
allows sunlight
to reach the forest floor.
Canopy gaps glisten into
plant growth
patterns.
Roots and moss interweave. I want
you to cut these pages
out. Tear them if
needed.

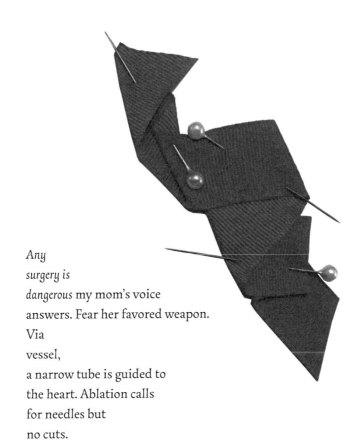

Any
surgery is
dangerous my mom's voice
answers. Fear her favored weapon.
Via
vessel,
a narrow tube is guided to
the heart. Ablation calls
for needles but
no cuts.

Debris
accumulates,
given as a glacier
advances. Crystal chandelier
tele-
graphing
light through an abandoned house. Though
glaciers seem motionless
their motion is
endless.

My mom's
memories mis-
match mine. I elide rooms
I ran from. She forgets hunger
and rage.
I lose
days, watch shattered glass reform as
twilight. Autumn didn't
seep through ductless
heat vents.

There are
many ways to
express pain, destruction
is just one of them. Hold your breath
then blow
it out.
I never hid myself in the
tall grass. I'm never scared.
I've never been
empty.

The weight
of a glacier
reshapes land. It carries
what it moves. Yes, sometimes my heart
beats too
fast and
blood rests on the surface of my
skin. I know this image.
Red leaves rain in
the street.

If I'm
haunted, then I'm
loved. Radio on. Bulb
flickering. A washcloth folded
square. Dark
matter
doesn't emit or interact
with light. It surrounds us
even if we can't
see it.

I have
fallen through ice.
I'm not the same, or where
I find myself isn't the same.
My dreams
change. In
car crashes, I wrap my body
like a halo around
yours to absorb
the harm.

Line's end;
or stone to mark
a boundary. I define
terminus in an attempt to
surface
grief, to
graft meaning. The elm I love is
cut apart by strangers.
They start with the
branches.

Glaciers
cycle from melt
to accumulation,
weathering into a flawless
surface.
Scatter
and re-gather the pages. Fold
them inside your books. Tuck
one in your breast
pocket.

In the
elm's place, we box
a garden in sunlight.
To forgive, you must reckon with
what's left.
Landforms
arise in two ways: land is stripped
away or is given
as a glacier
retreats.

As you
form a sense of
self, you recognize that
you're separate from everything. You
mirror
me, and
I mirror you. Our lungs feel the
trees. We share symmetry;
it reminds us
we're real.

Agate
picked from gravel
to cover your eyes. We
don't experience time as a
line. The
people
I've been and the fires I'll tend creep
out of me. I'm not sure
I can even
stop them.

Because
I need something,
wind along grain silos,
40-second mimic of waves
in a
loop. In
every bird's belly there's plastic.
Cut open any bird.
The glaciers will
vanish.

She tears
the bark from a
maple in strips. I watch
for symptoms and try to reset
my heart-
beat. The
phlebotomist draws vials. The
surgeon waits to set fire
to tissue and
stitch scars.

Scans showed
ablation was
not safe for my mom's heart
because the defect occurred too
near her
heart's nerve
center, the sinoatrial
node. There are parts of the
heart that can't be
removed.

Destroy
the defect and
risk obliterating
the center. So the defect lurked
coiled snake,
broken
limb, lightning fissure, ice compressed
to crystal. Glaciers form
when snow remains
the same.

Trauma
passes across
generations. This is
what's meant by circulatory
system.
Before
birth, my body felt my mom's pain.
I recall her life, store
her hurt in dark
corners.

Soundscape
as offering,
the tremendous ache of
ice that cracks and settles hollow
and deep
in my
chest cavity. The echo is
in me, but you can't
hear it past the
static.

I'm just
a pattern of
cells trying to heal through
repetition. It's easy to
become
nothing.
It's easy to speak softly and
shadow by, guttering
like a waking
nightmare.

Keening
of flowers. The
chop and hum of blades in
the heart of a machine. What I
suffer
trembles
when faced with what my mom endured.
Battered body. Mute voice.
Rape a bitter
wellspring.

Whispers
swell into a
low moan. Your life is
the gift of our will to survive.
I'd break
glass and
swallow smoke for you. She'd tear her
last dollar in half, cross
plains to help you
escape.

I eat
paper and vow
never to take the same
route. A river will sharpen to
cut through
its own
curve and form a new path. Agnes
Martin said *we give up*
things that cover
our mind.

White fades
to blue near a
glacier's terminus. Skin
wears the landscape inside its cells.
Latticed
organ
like a flower opening or
a wound, water is meant
to catch and break
the light.

In the
end it's her heart
only indirectly.
Pulmonary embolism,
a clot
lodged in
the lungs. When the air holds me, I
recognize the same arms,
body that was
my home.

Plasma
transfusion. Bring
up bilirubin. Room
5th floor. Steroids counteract dye.
Ultra-
sound down
the throat. Iodine. CT scan.
Coumadin level. I've
made myself a
clearing.

Take out
garbage. Fridge stuff/
Bread. Bananas. Meds? ~~Mail?~~
Clothes. Jogging pants. Sweatshirts.
Little
suitcase.
Denture stuff. Diapers. Unders. Socks.
Follow the crease where the
envelope meets
itself.

Plasma
Transfusion
"Sodium"
dye
Bring ⊘steroids
up
Bilirubin contrast dye
612-273-3000

CT scan

Coumadin
Level
down to
1.

Bruce - 5th floor
Room 505A
U-2 floor

ultrasound
down the
throat.

(meds?)

Bananas

take out garbage

fridge stuff / Bread

mail?

clothes
Jogging pants
Sweatshirts
Undees
Socks
Desitine stuff
Diapers
little suit case.

Some days
I'm made of bone.
Other days I'm made of
water. Some days I've got no skin
and tears
pour from
my eyes and spill over my hands
as I rinse jars for jam.
Some days I've got
no words.

I try
not to count the
beta blockers she took
to calm her heart. I try not to
count each
worthless
pill. Glaciers flow like very slow
rivers. Every place I
love was covered
in ice.

Every
place I love was
carved open by moving
water my chest echoes. I can't
tell you
what it
means. I can't tell you what it is
to hold love and hurt in
the same organ.
I can't.

Loss starts
to burnish me
smooth. *Impenetrable*
matter stripped to encounter. Stone,
stone, we
are tied
to each other /while we exist.
What breaks breaks so let it
disintegrate
with you.

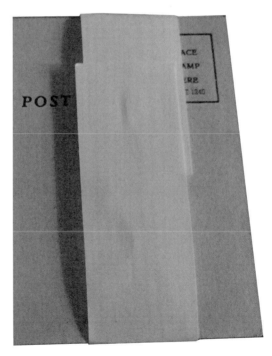

I sew
love into your
jacket where the fabric
hems into itself in seams. The
grass shifts
slip for
slip, a hologram redoubling
its image so that each
piece remembers
the whole.

You are
already a
part of me, crucial like
a ribcage. Carnations unfold
to white,
curling
outward from the heart. Rearrange
the text to claim it, then
heal the pages
with thread.

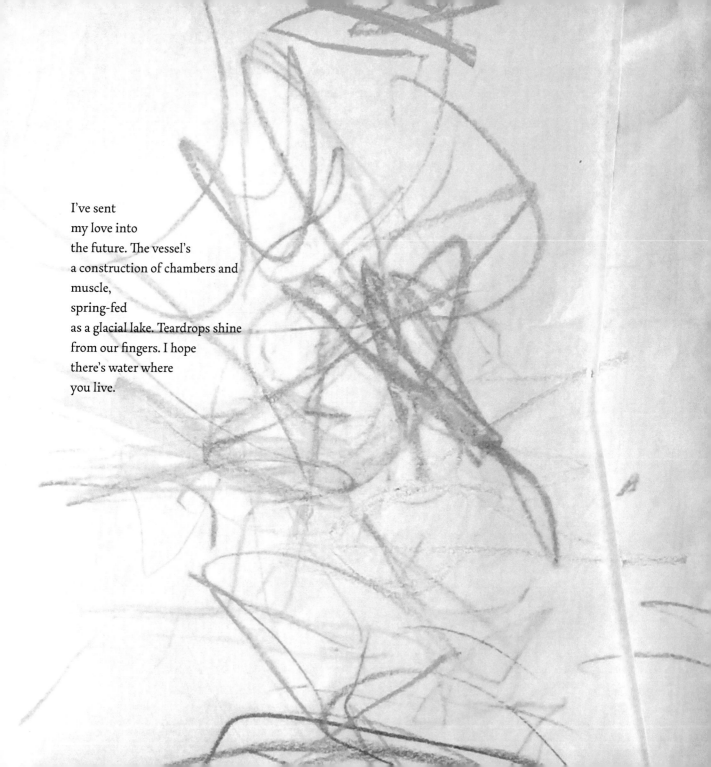

I've sent
my love into
the future. The vessel's
a construction of chambers and
muscle,
spring-fed
as a glacial lake. Teardrops shine
from our fingers. I hope
there's water where
you live.

The rain we ache for falls in a veil. The sun breaks the clouds
as we stop on the shoulder of County Hwy 8. We're placed
on the parcel scrawled "Wogenson" in land tracts my brother
unearthed. Mom's grandparents claimed this farm, now diminished,
when they emigrated from Denmark.

A stand of pines obscures
the house. It's painted dark green as though it might disperse
into the landscape. This place I can't quite see. Place she wasn't
allowed to touch most things. Spun glass and woven tapestries.

Place where, as a girl, she was made to finish every bite down to
the dab of unused ketchup. Waste not. Did these grandparents
predict her life's unfurling, its tendriled want? Days she starved herself
until she shook. The night she beat her small boy, this same brother,
not yet 6, for eating every hot dog meant for dinner cold, out of hunger.

She would not stop hitting him. Because there was no money for more food. I remember the shape of her want engulfed us in billowing sweetness.

I don't remember my mom's
grandmother—a woman who wouldn't or couldn't be a shield—
beyond an antique smell, proxy memory of the dainty napkins
I inherited with edges tatted robin's egg blue. At the highway's edge,
I'm warmed by unexpected godlight and a field of wildflowers.

The most I hoped for was a quiet ditch of sharpened grass.

I wade waist-deep in yellow flowers–Echinacea Paradoxa,
Coneflower, Black-Eyed Susan—untwist a plastic pouch
and release ash and chipped bone. My mom becomes a memory
of the flowers.
                        I don't know where our people are buried.

Across the street, an apiary. The bees are asleep in their boxes.

I Make Lists.

I name what I need to remember:

She had beautiful hands, piano player's fingers,
nails neatly trimmed to ovals, never squared.

On principle, she refused bangs or to crop her hair
above the shoulder. I ran my hands through it.

She once stapled the hem of her dress
because she never learned to sew.

She cherished antique objects, particularly
coverworn books and decorative tins.

As a child she adored the most unlovable candy:
circus peanuts. She hated fruit-flavored anything.

She didn't have a favorite color; she claimed
whatever color was favored by her current lover.

Playing hide-the-thimble, she put a green thimble
on her nose–one origin of my love of thimbles.

The snick of her air hockey wrist was unrivaled;
she wouldn't insult you by letting you win.

She sliced tomatoes, then shimmered them
with salt or with sugar in equal measure.

Her voice had a dulcet rasp. There's no one
I'd rather hear sing except, perhaps, my daughter.

She called that daughter, her youngest
granddaughter, *my little beauty.*

She taught her how to palm a rock
and release it so it skips across water.

I engage in magical thinking:

Her heart kept beating.

The clot didn't dislodge.

She quit smoking.

She went to the hospital.

She said her heart hurt.

She had money to go to the doctor.

One health insurance plan was enough.

She told me she'd been so tired.

- Kyle → lists are automatically cynical.

Lyn Hejinian + Anne Boyer Vocabulary 4/15/21
reading series

- ▣ Betelgeuse (star) disappeared? (Anne Boyer poem refs).
- ▣ merciless to (hear) out loud
  " merciless to read out loud" Lyn on "Fail Creek"

Paula Generative WS 4/16/21

- Space hurricane
- map-inspired playlist
- 7 PM Sunday rdg. Diane Seuss
- Robert Pogue Harrison — book about tree/ human relationship
- Brainstorm: stages of grief no one tells you about

But the universe is lost + open, multi-diamond front

space time flattens out into a black hole? flatness

it only temporarily

imitation

relief like light

dreams in which I am her voice

dreams of her unable to speak

Grief

dreams of her mouth stuffed w/ felt

obsperation

distances opening

dreams of her mother

dreams of her living

see also: black field

dreams of her weeping

other distances closing

dreams of her sleeping

and all of it clear. all of it coalescing

my grief + yours +

see also

mother-solving, death-solving

I make a list of things I don't know:

      The source of the clot.

      How long and what route it took.

      What pain she felt.

      Whether she lay in bed afraid to move.

      If she knew she was going to die.

      When she knew she was going to die.

I make a list of things I know:

Her clothes still hang in her closet.

The paperwork in boxes
piled a mess only she could decipher.

I keep a recording of her voice
mostly for the sound of her laugh.

Her eyes were gold-flecked green.

Her skin smelled like her.

Her clothes still do.

I see her in lichen and feel her
move leaves.

She's in the chlorophyll
in the grass and the trees,
in the light and anything it grows.

I miss her and wish her peace
swift as her heart.

Center

Karl-Anthony Towns, center for the Minnesota Timberwolves, experienced unfathomable loss in a span of months. His mother, Jacqueline Cruz-Towns, died from complications caused by COVID-19 on April 13th, 2020. Subsequently that year, Towns' family lost six more loved ones to the disease.

In a December 2020 post-game interview, Towns is thoughtful and unguarded, as though his insides are obsidian. Speaking of himself in the past tense, he says, *that Karl died on April 13th. He's never coming back. I don't remember that man. I don't know that man.*

I'm volcanic glass when I say, *I'll never be the same. None of us will be the same. We no longer exist. Our mothers leave us obsidian* we'll need to lean into a microphone without her. I didn't understand mother-shaped chasms until July opened mine.

That woman meant the world to me. More than y'all will ever know and write…It's such a different pain than even y'all recognize, Towns says to unseen reporters.

My mom told a story about my birth. The doctor handed my dad scissors to cut the umbilical cord. My dad hesitated, paled, shook his head and handed the scissors back. Later, my mom asked my dad if he'd been squeamish about the blood. *No.* He couldn't sever the line that tied her life to mine. He couldn't bear the weight of it.

A gold heart on a chain rests against Towns' chest throughout *The Toughest Year of My Life*, the documentary he created to honor his mother. The loss of her *is something that's not describable.* The weight disappears with her.

Though her body was unrecognizable in a coma, Towns says of his mother, *I could feel her energy. It's something a mother—a mother and a child connection that just can never be misplaced. We speak telepathically.* The doctors, *they didn't feel it, but I felt it.*

After an ambling June day in 2018, I went into active labor when I lay down to nap. The on-call doctor at my OBGYN's office said, *You're fine. Wait an hour and call back.* Immediately after I hung up, my mom called. She heard my voice. *Go now, honey. This baby is coming.* My husband drove us the 10 minutes to the hospital. My water broke as I entered the triage room.

I don't even recognize most of my other games and years I've played and how I felt those days.

I recall how it felt to be a person with a mother, but I no longer recognize that person as myself. I lost her like we lose days, each moment as it passes.

To say it's been day-by-day is probably an understatement. I think it's been more moment by moment.

We move through moments. We begin to heal as we can and must, but we'll never be the same.

For months after my mom died, friends tell me, *you're made of strong stuff*. Obsidian is volcanic glass formed when lava cools rapidly with minimal crystal growth. Obsidian is brittle and can't be carved, but when chipped can be sharper than surgical steel. Obsidian is from my mom. Sometimes because she gave it from what was best in her. Sometimes because I sourced a blade to protect myself from what was worst in her.

At the press conference, when asked by a reporter how he got through the game, Towns takes a long pause, holds space, shakes his head softly as he considers how best to state what no one can understand exactly but himself. *When you, um, being honest, when you go through what I've been through, you just find a different source of strength. I don't know how to explain it...*

The Towns family celebrates what should've been Jacqueline's 59th birthday, unfurling red and gold and green confetti against an unapologetically blue sky.

The same July sky my mom died beneath a week later.

Field

My mother is a nebula. My mother's eyes are closed
like she's already a ghost. An exoskeleton twins her.
She collapses time. I never called her my mother.

My mother isn't inside the car but neither is she
outside the car. Dust disperses. Her hand clutches
the door. Her hand clutches the door with devotion

and necessity. Her love has painted the body in two-
toned blue. You can't see it, but the car's backseat is raw
unupholstered metal. Memory is a host. My dead live

here in a corridor of rust thatched together in a
ramshackle structure. The grass is overgrown.
When my mother is pregnant, her voice refracts

against porcelain as she spills outward. Her scales
feather the drain. Seeds spread. The home we left
is a field. I watch the field dismantle the shack,

swallow rust. My mother clutches the car's door
as though it's what keeps her upright, what keeps her
from collapsing, what keeps her from vanishing.

Remember the quiet evenings. My mother is liminal.
My mother is cleft, between worlds. She speaks to me.
She speaks to me from a mouth filled with clover.

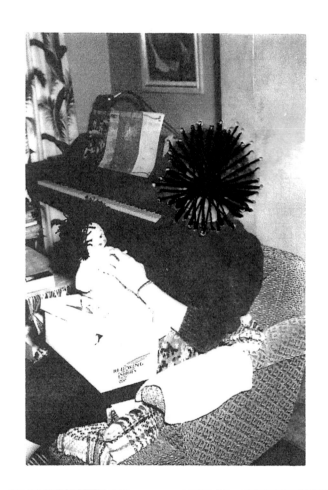

The Nothing

The nothing wears a flaming crown.

The nothing drinks Zima.

The nothing knocks on my sister's door and climbs into her,
lungs-first.

The nothing slips my brother a knife.

The nothing gives my brother a wife.

I swallow scarves for the nothing and pull
them from my throat, relentless.

The nothing breaks horses
gagged with spit-slick metal bits.

The nothing's got the gold fever.

The nothing drives a white Lincoln Town Car
with a burgundy leather interior.

The nothing accumulates 8 DUIs and 7 ex-
spouses, sons-of-bitches to a number.

The nothing pulls you into this world
with forceps.

The nothing boils hot dog water for gravy.

The nothing's outside the bathroom door
when my mom's father puts his dick in her 3-year-old hands.

The nothing jams balled up socks in her mouth.

The nothing ignores her muffled screams
when her stepfather rapes her at 15.

The nothing marks you for future abuse
and then abandons you.

The nothing bruises your body and forgets.

The nothing survives being doused in gasoline.

The nothing palms my matches.

The nothing snuffs faces
from photographs.

The nothing keeps a list of atrocities
and abominations; mountain lions:
they're on the list.

The nothing is an adherent of trench warfare.

The nothing carries a baseball bat.

The nothing files frivolous lawsuits and wins.

The nothing takes the money.

The nothing takes the money.

The nothing always takes the money.

The nothing haunts me down several highways.

You wake up in a cold sweat next to the nothing
outside a carnival in Florida.

The nothing applies its face before a lighted mirror.

The nothing bathes in baby oil.

The nothing plays "In Heaven There Is No Beer"
on an omnichord during the witching hour.

The nothing hits a royal flush and fans the money
before you on matted carpeting.

The nothing safeguards an antique harmonica
in a puzzle box.

The nothing plucks its eyebrows to wisps.

The nothing values thinness.

The nothing eats little.

The nothing lets you starve yourself.

The nothing blacks out and spins nests from sugar.

Having been beautiful, the nothing covets beauty.

The nothing perches on a cushion.

The greatest injustice is that you cannot outlive the nothing.

The nothing emerges from the desert half wraith.

The nothing bears its own fist-shaped wounds.

The nothing's carpal bones are fused at the wrist.

The nothing walks quietly.
The nothing builds terrariums.

May we all have the grit to openly drag the boat motors
of our would-be rapists across their lawns and into our garages
tarnished in starlight like the nothing.

The nothing scrubs floors on padded knees.

The nothing perfects bread.

The nothing perfects pie crusts.

If a dish comes out imperfect, it goes in the trash;
the nothing accepts no objections.

The nothing coats twigs and pine cones
in metallic spray paint for meticulous crafts
you're not invited to partake in.

The nothing excels at Tiddlywinks.

The nothing sends you home with French toast and jam
to feed you for weeks.

The nothing will not abide you drinking coffee
reheated in a microwave.

The nothing tells you you're descended from Danish royalty,
the Dark Danes.

The nothing keeps a tidy house.

The nothing gnashes its teeth.

The nothing wears a mouth guard to bed.

The nothing drinks alone in the pines.

The nothing nurses delusions of grandeur.

The nothing does not wish to be called what it is.

The nothing has business ideas.

The nothing is flanked by German shepherds.

The nothing cages a bluebird of happiness.

I try to dispel the nothing by changing my name.

The nothing once sang in a country western band.

The nothing bequeaths you a lacquered guitar.
The nothing is a gifted raconteur.

The nothing leaves cigarettes burning.
The nothing cries only for itself.

The nothing clutches at a gold crucifix around its neck.

Phantom Thread

My mom didn't like to be looked at. She pulled away when I rested my head against her breast. She hated her misused body. I understand that she was how she was because she'd been touched when she shouldn't have been touched. She saw herself distorted in mirrors. She saw herself in a girl in my 6th grade class, Chelsea of the serious face. *She's a little touched,* my mom said. No one ever touched me, though I feel as though they might have. I felt her terror through my life.

My mom loved to save living things. When I was 6, after a neighbor poisoned our dog with antifreeze as retribution for chasing pheasants in his field, we adopted a golden retriever named Cassie Rose who'd been beaten severely by her previous owner. Cassie was terrified to enter the house and wouldn't leave the kitchen. My mom sat on the floor across from her all night and spoke softly, coaxed the dog into inching on her belly across the floor.

Later, my mom looked after two small children, Billie and her brother, whose name I can't recall. I recall the pain of witnessing the palpable relief they felt entering our house, the relief of temporary safety. I recall the cigarette burns in their flesh, the way the wide pools of their eyes over-compensated for their difficulty speaking. She reported the abuse to the county, but nothing changed. *I couldn't save them,* she said, and regretted it all her life.

My mom was a marvel in an emergency. She knew just what to say in the rest area parking lot after my brother's roommates called me to collect him, when he'd been burning and cutting into his skin. She knew just what to say while the rest of us cowered, afflicted in the face of his hurt. She knew just how to enfold him in her arms. Some small shade in me still yearns to be sick, because it's the only time I feel worthy of being cared for.

Swallowtail.

If you cannot cry, ask
what is wrong with your body.

— Han VanderHart, *What Pecan Light*

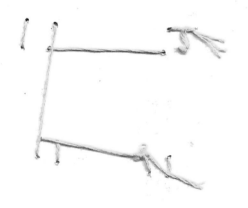

On the bank of the river we love through our lives,
a black swallowtail alights on a ditch flower.

My daughter's arms circle her torso in joy of fastening boots.
In her swaying, she strikes my neck, hard. Tears well in my eyes,
because I can't remember the last time someone hit me. I don't
remember being a person hit by someone she loved until I'm
struck again. I can't describe the feeling. In my mind, with language,
I don't remember being hit. But my body remembers.

Black swallowtail | yellow swallowtail, envoy of symmetry.

When my sister was the same age as my daughter,
she hurled a tumbler into the heart of a low, square table
with a glass top. The table was beloved by her dad, my stepdad,
and, consequently, beloved by our mom, particularly after
my stepdad died in a head-on collision with a semi-truck

while driving home from work. | The tabletop shattered.

The physical violence wasn't as bad as the turning away,
the guttural sound in her throat when she tore us in strips.
I have a voice that was only for my mom. Pleading, conciliatory,

asleep at the wheel. | I'd forgotten swallowtails exist.

I can't cry observed. I shade my eyes, move to corners.
I excuse myself, leave rooms and close doors. I keen into
bedspreads, hangered jackets, wadded towels.

His stomach was in his throat. | I didn't know swallowtails could be black.

Are you happy, my girl asks, *are you happy?* The square of glass too dear, the table was never made whole.

The river rolls its stone into kettles. | Stone carves the kettles.

The kettles are carved in stone.

Doubting Thomas.

I search for my grief and feel relief when it surfaces. You must touch the wound to believe it exists.

You drop my brother in the dirt. You leave the brother I pulled from the water in the driveway, spilled on his side, weeping. You leave your 9-year-old son to cry into the earth.

You're incredulous. Your eyes gape. You can't believe unless your hand reaches to widen the wound that widens your eyes.

It's cold when the chasm you dread spreads its breath across the wind-shield. I carve letters backwards in the fog. I carve the letters backwards so we can read them from outside.

You weren't there to witness. You weren't there to see the print of nails. In examining the wound, you enter darkness. You become faithless.

A good pattern, a pattern who allows, a pattern who can't or won't speak. My brother becomes you, will-less. We're locked in our patterns.

You keep a letter I don't remember writing. You keep a letter in which I pledge fealty to stability. The choice lanced a wound in my side, a gash unsubsiding.

If you can't bear to cut the children in half, let the children decide where to halve themselves.

Aug. 15, 1992

Dear Judge James R. Clifford,

This letter concerns the case of
Thomas A. Stegeman vs. Cammy M. Stegeman
whom of which are my Parents. I am ten years
of age. My brothers Michael and Christopher XXX are
eight and six XXX I request to live with our father
Thomas A. Stegeman.

Sincerly,

Danika K. Stegeman

Relentless.

To survive, you became relentless with yourself.

I scrub the baseboards until skin peels from my fingers, relentless.

I crack my knuckles when interrupted, relentless.

I count ounces, relentless.

I tick syllables, relentless.

I clench my teeth, relentless.

I dissect my grief, relentless.

I rake leaves until my back bows, then brace my pregnant body against a chair to cross the room, relentless.

I pick at my face until my bones ache, relentless.

I worry stones, relentless.

I hold my breath, relentless.

I black out, relentless.

I lose hours, relentless.

I lure demons just to starve them, relentless.

I plot escape routes from moving vehicles, swelling crowds, burning houses, relentless.

The first draft of my first book was an island of couplets that became menacing in its uniformity, relentless.

I'm a contortionist, relentless.

I'll fill out your court forms and government documents, relentless.

Black and white thinking is a coping strategy that can become maladaptive and no longer serve the trauma survivor, relentless.

I tackle friends into cars, relentless.

I anticipate the needs of others, relentless.

I give unsolicited advice, relentless.

I transform desire into action, relentless.

I'm a chariot, relentless.

I'll tell you where to step and how to speak, relentless.

My grocery list follows the floor plan of the store, relentless.

I reposition the orange juice behind the Brita pitcher, relentless.

Towels must be folded long side first, short side second, relentless.

Each dish is strategically placed, relentless.

I make reservations I regret, relentless.

I chart moon phases, relentless.

I plan funerals, relentless.

I white-knuckle my tender contents through snowstorms to reach you, relentless.

During a performance review, I ask my supervisor *in what universe am I not exceptional?*, relentless.

I compare my being to the body of the crucifixion of Christ, relentless.

I scrape skin from my brother's slender ribs dragging him from the lazy river, relentless.

The brother I didn't pull from the water says the Joy Division song "She's Lost Control" is about me, relentless.

I couldn't trust the people who created my life, so anyone and no one can be trusted, relentless.

I'm clinging to the nearest passerby, relentless.

No minor shift in my periphery or your fascia goes unseen and uncatalogued, relentless.

I shear through sheaths of tissue you think you hide in, relentless.

I prefer the company of trees, relentless.

The person who held me until I fell asleep was the same person who left me in the care of strangers for hours into the night so she could buy drugs, relentless.

A 10-year-old girl carrying the delicate weight of my infant sister against my shoulder, I paced the hallway, relentless.

At 8 I begged the grocer for scraps of bread and a package of Carl Buddig lunch meat, relentless.

I bruise fruit, relentless.

I key cars, relentless.

I set fires, relentless.

I cradle a tequila bottle and ghostride hotel elevators floor to floor, relentless.

I shatter glass, relentless.

I piece shards, relentless.

I cull the fold, relentless.

I live in an open field, relentless.

I'll repopulate your wasteland with native flora and fauna, relentless.

I strip gristle and fat from still-warm flesh, relentless.

I knew if I wanted anything good in my life I'd have to make it myself, my mom says, and I understand that she gave me what allowed me to survive her, relentless.

If the text must be corporeal, I must insist on its being vaginal, relentless.

I must insist on cunnilingus, relentless.

If we have to name the animals and other totems, I'll have to insist on gender neutral and/or feminine pronouns, relentless.

I sing "Knife Party" by the Deftones while brandishing the biggest chef's knife in the knife block, relentless.

I break rules, relentless.

I beg forgiveness, relentless.

No one is one thing or another but everything at once, relentless.

I spiral like a galaxy, relentless.

I swarm like starlings, relentless.

I'll repeat myself until you hear me, relentless.

I spread coal-dark roots to anchor me upright, relentless.

I hoard my horrors in the half-forgotten husks of viceroys, relentless.

I swallow your debt and emerge triumphant from its depths, relentless.

I intend to win at all costs, relentless.

I vomit in your lap mid-sentence, relentless.

I consider fileting the flesh from my body in strips in a clawfoot bathtub, relentless.

I experience difficulties differentiating my feelings from the feelings of others, relentless.

I lie through my teeth to please you, relentless.

We're all basically anorexic, relentless.

I deny the mind what it desires, relentless.

I bask in what the mind desires, relentless.

I devour self-help tomes, relentless.

I weep through yoga sessions, relentless.

I'm humbled before the divinity of your panentheistic nature deities, relentless.

I transmute pain into fury, relentless.

I transmogrify what's destroyed me into what sustains me, relentless.

I skinslip from self to self, relentless.

I regard your inability to hold space for raw emotion as cowardice, relentless.

I resent your deep-seated fears as failures of the spirit, relentless.

My childhood friends hang themselves from stark trees when the solstice can't return the light fast enough, relentless.

I've got angels destroyed in car crashes, relentless.

I've got angels who scratch at their faces, relentless.

I panic, relentless.

I clutch a wooden spoon for the seizures, relentless.

I rush from stairway to stairway, relentless.

The rage that lives in my body might fuel a small planet, relentless.

I sigh to keep my breath moving, relentless.

I tether my core to the core of the earth, relentless.

I'll bear the grief of others like a reservoir, relentless.

The river is ravenous, relentless.

The forest is ravenous, relentless.

Where is your mother?, relentless.

I sew over faces, over wildflowers with thread, relentless.

I whisper into paper folds, relentless.

I doze in a chair at the bedside of your dislocated bones, relentless.

I allow my intuition to flow through me, relentless.

I unfurl energy in coils, relentless.

I carry burdens across decades to lay them at your feet, relentless.

A mother-eating presence manifests in my house, relentless.

I swallow nettles, relentless.

I dispel a hail of needles, relentless.

When the goddess approaches, she wears the face and feathers of a crow, relentless.

A woman is ash, a woman is without time, relentless.

I fill notebooks with imaginary birds, relentless.

I possess a healing machine, relentless.

I die to the past every moment, relentless.

I'll keep you safe, sweetheart, relentless.

I fall to my knees in the hedges behind the car wash, relentless.

When I say God I mean a field of energy, relentless.

When Leonard Cohen says the stars eat your body, he means the stars eat your body, relentless.

We're alive in the world at the same time, relentless.

I ask questions because I don't know the answers, relentless.

I salvage brick, relentless.

I trim wicks, relentless.

I kiss bejeweled lips, relentless.

I'll make the ring fit, relentless.

I'm filled with a depthless longing, relentless.

I can't be here in my body, relentless.

I watch you craft ghosts from pantyhose and poly-fil on a loop, relentless.

I bathe in patchouli and bath salts, relentless.

My blood pressure is a study in diminishing returns, relentless.

I ingest arctic root extracts to dampen my nervous system's hypersensitivity to external stressors daily, relentless.

I disintegrate with minimal provocation, relentless.

I etch my list of minerals into a meteorite, relentless.

Sirens sound, relentless.

Crows call, relentless.

Falcons hunt the freeways, relentless.

Moss lines the subways, relentless.

Watch the rail shine, relentless.

Throw rugs writhe in a simulacra of ferns and palm fronds, relentless.

The universe unfastens in infinite permutations, relentless.

The body is an animal that desires survival, relentless.

I wash menstrual blood from my hands, relentless.

I fill my cup, relentless.

I fill my cup to brimming, relentless.

A primordial void pools at the base of my spinal cord, relentless.

I open portals I can't close, relentless.

The eye is lidless, relentless.

The eye unhinges, relentless.

The eye is an electric cell, relentless.

Restring me like pearls, relentless.

Soak my brother in water when his bone growth outpaces his muscles to aching, relentless.

Soak my brother in alcohol, relentless.

Dress my sister in wisps of smoke, relentless.

We're a haunted people, relentless.

Where is the mother of your body?, relentless.

Is your goddess a black hole like mine?, relentless.

Compaction is a force that increases a core's density via compression, relentless.

Manifestation is a force that confesses a core's destiny via accretion, relentless.

Any act of creation is simultaneously an act of annihilation, relentless.

I turn to prayer, relentless.

I turn from prayer, relentless.

I negate the nothing, relentless.

I'm trying to heal into surrender, relentless.

I expect disaster, relentless.

I brace myself, relentless.

I wash dishes by hand because a vessel is a promise, relentless.

A vessel is a lesson in release, relentless.

I know a woman who shovels sugarcane waste and shreds plastic for paper fibers, relentless.

I know a woman who washes plagues from textiles, relentless.

I know a woman who darns holes into wholeness, relentless.

I know my body is a vessel, my home is a vessel, my daughter is a vessel, my mouth is a vessel, my mother is a vessel, my vocabulary is a vessel, my double is a vessel, my heart is a vessel spilling, relentless.

The fields are vessels, the silos are vessels, the clouds are vessels, relentless.

Time is a vessel, relentless.

A seed is a vessel, a bridge is a vessel, relentless.

What do you carry?, relentless.

What do you carry that you can't let go of?, relentless.

What lives in your body?, relentless.

I know waiting is a kind of prayer, relentless.

I let the scales fall from my eyes, relentless.

I vanish into the foreground, relentless.

It can only come in if you invite it in, relentless.

Field

for the brother I didn't pull from the water

The social worker can't remember your name when he brings you out so I can bring you home. We get in the car, and the car's garbage. We walk into my house, and the house and everything inside it's garbage. You decide not to live there, so you live outside for a while.

I go to the mall, and everything is garbage. Everyone wears layers to protect themselves. I eat Domino's Pizza at a birthday party and think, *I'm eating garbage. I'm putting garbage into my body.* The pile of gifts and the papers and plastics they're wrapped in are garbage too.

I watch TV, and it's garbage. Everything's awful with being looked at. I look at your face. It looks miserable and not like you at all. I remember when your body was the same as a horse's body. A soft kind of ease purled through you like muscle. What lives in your body now hurts.

You punch the glass out of a window pane, and it's garbage. You cut your hand, and the black stitches sewn into it are garbage. The nurse sets each stitch she threads free into the garbage. The day after, we try to go to the place our lives broke, but it's just an empty field. It's sort of merciful.

We Can't Afford Horses

We can't afford horses. What makes the sentence
compelling is the double "or" sound. The narrow-
entranced cave of the mouth echoes the sentiment of lack
expressed in the terse, unadorned statement. This is how
my poet heart works: intuit the right mouth sounds, repeat.
This is how once we did have a horse. How he cost $100.
How I wished on a falling star for a pony and got
a full-grown Appaloosa. How his markings were mottled
red-brown on white. How his mane grew in red-black shocks.
How he'd only abide being ridden bareback. How our dad
led us around on the horse's back in winter. How we fell
to the snow, braced and deafened by the cold beside
his unmoving hooves. How we never rode him again,
but washed and brushed his sweet-smelling frame,
his scent of woods and dried hay. How we brewed
his trough into a stew of twigs and pine cones.
How we didn't name him; how his name was a joke
between our mom and the nothing. How the nothing
hand-chose him at a horse auction and then failed
to break him. How next a roughrider tried to break him,
but the horse rolled on the rider's body, bloodlust in his
embered eyes. How he barreled through barbed wire
to run. How, buckled in the car's backseat, we chased him
down gravel roads at a full gallop. How we fingered his cuts
with salve. How he forced open the gate the day he was to be
sold. How our dad told the buyer the kids set the horse loose.
How it must've sounded true because the buyer took him away.
How I'd later ride a horse in Costa Rica, tell a horsewoman
who knew better that I knew horses. How she paired me
with a spirited stallion. How he smelled rust and unease.
How he ran to the head of the line of horses and tired himself.

How the guides, whose language I didn't share, laughed at me,
but gently. How we lagged behind on the way back,
just him and me and a narrow track, the horse worn down.
How he reared to toss me, but, by some fluke, I held tight.

Heart Rate

Cento

in the construction of the chest there is a heart

and I am aware of my heart: it opens and closes
its bowl of red blooms out of sheer love of me

I cannot heave my heart into my mouth

of the heart they say too much the heart the heart

I'm terrified at the moral apathy–the death of the
heart–which is happening here in my country

to further compromise an already compromised heart

a heart that's full up like a landfill

deep in the heart of the land

look into the dark heart and you will see what the dark eats
other than your heart

the actual heart is an ugly machine

it doesn't stir the heart like a true wild rose

admit that the heart, though not useless, lacks the thing needed
for some miracles

I had a friend whose heart was too heavy to hold,
yes there's blood on the median like a boat without oars

nobody broke your heart, you broke your own

Heart Rate Variability is shaped by trauma

oh yeah I, I got a heart of darkness

won't you feel for me from your heart

there in your heart something that's never changing

it's time to decide while my heart mourns

I sit heart-stricken at the bloom

in between a heart and home

today I will say my fears into a molting bag
and let them mean away in there as doom means doom
and love means love when I'm waiting here
calibrating my heart

I found your beating heart half-buried in the woods

yardsale heart just like mine

i carry your heart with me(i carry it in my heart)

crowned in our sins, velvet hearts

and you kept us awake with wolves' teeth
sharing different heartbeats

lay your head where my heart used to be

and I will remove the heart of stone from your flesh
and give you a heart of flesh

heart we will forget

some relaxed uncondescending stranger,
the heart's release, and while the fireflies are failing
to illuminate these nightmare trees

leave my heart down by the water

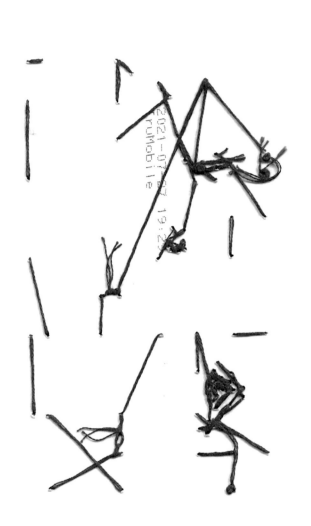

I didn't know how to write about home until I left. The smell of home as I leave the plane to enter the jet bridge is the smell of fresh water. Glaciers faltered through and opened thousands upon thousands of lakes. If we don't have enough water to produce adequate rainfall, what happens everywhere else?

We felled the pine forests. My friend lives north where owls watch fires and wolves mourn for moonlight. She tells me about the Lost 40, a surveyor's error that constructed a mirage of lake where in fact there lay virgin woods. Walking in, she felt haunted. The overgrowth was tangled, the trees otherworldly.

In Sandstone, the town where my mom left her body, the dredged and forking trails are gone, but near the river logging camp ghosts linger. The river flooded with timber the current couldn't clear. Men with hooks and prods were crushed freeing wood to water. Pine needles soften the strata of industry.

A giving stone, ease in carving paired with grit and glitter, made sandstone a desirable building material. Quarry work left slabs of stacked stone with vertical rivulets from drill bits cleft into the rock faces. Grand halls in St. Paul are still supported by pillars of Kettle River sandstone. The river is rust-colored. Its bed is dappled with voids of varying sizes.

As kids, we wandered the mossy hollows and echoing caves. Once, we found the skinned carcass of a small cat, eyeless and slit from belly to throat. We'd heard rumors of devil worship in the caves and on the river's banks—missing dogs hung on nooses of bailing twine—but had never witnessed direct evidence. I experienced waking nightmares, recurring intrusive images of the sacrifice.

Quit being such a mother hen, my aunt scolded on the hike, before we found the cat. A sense of peril grasped my hand and walked beside me, a pervasive low-lying cloud of dread. I understood at all times that I wasn't safe. I tried desperately to protect the people I loved with what magic, dark or light, I could muster.

I tell an acquaintance where I'm from, and he responds that the most horrific story he's ever heard is how parents tried to save their children from The Great Hinckley Fire by enclosing their bodies in metal barrels. The implication of his admission is a depthless misery as the flame walls encroached and barrel turned from shield to oven.

Hinckley Elementary School asked my 6th grade class to draw a coloring book in remembrance of the fire, as a rite of passage, as posterity for the future, because mine was the class of 2000, a new millennium, a new dream. My assigned page illustrated Skunk Lake: families huddled beneath swamp-drenched wool blankets, terrified livestock, engulfed timber all around. A train loaded with frantic people screamed up along the water's edge, its wheels and windows ablaze. As a teenager, I rode my bike past Skunk Lake on the ghosted line of railroad tracks paved into a trail. That lake is a glorified pond of knee-deep, muck-bottomed water.

The casino opened, and the town built around the train depot turned fire museum deteriorated, building by boarded building. The Dairy Queen moved to the freeway, became a hair salon my mom nicknamed The Hairy Queen, and then nothing. Grass grows through the cracks in the sidewalks along main street.

I used to call the operator on the pay phone across the street from the museum and ask for the time, just to hear the operator's voice and the click as she disconnected the line, the clink of my dime returned to me.

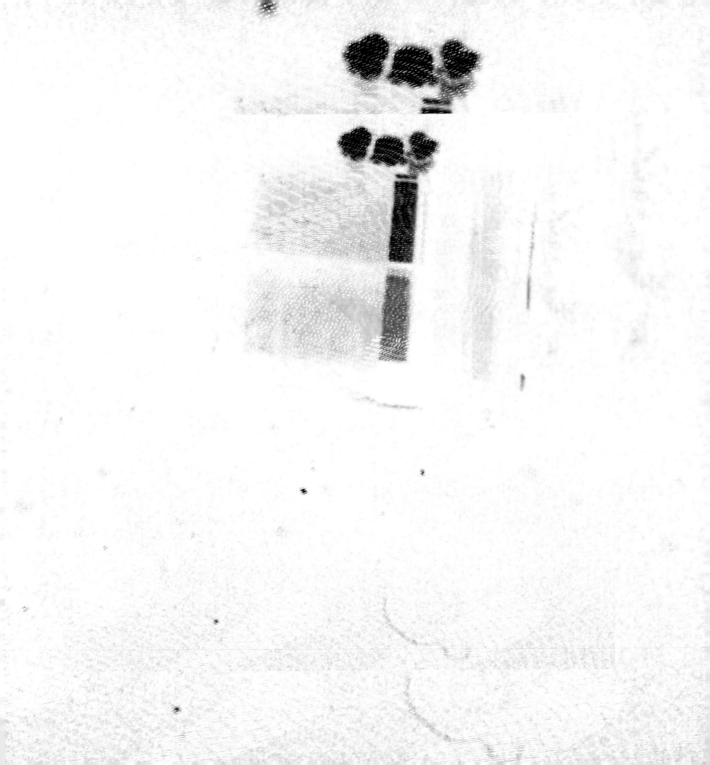

Notes.

The italicized words in the dedication are from the Sparklehorse song "Gold Day."

"I mouth the word motherless": "I feel like 1000 dead birds" is my brother Mike's line. "Dust in my heart, wind in my hair" is a mishearing of the lyrics "The dust in my head / The wind in my heart" from "Listening Wind" by Talking Heads.

"Ablation": The italicized lines in "[Loss starts / to burnish me…]" are George Oppen's and the whole sequence and probably everything I do is influenced by Oppen's poetry. The sequence is also influenced by Agnes Martin's gridwork and Emily Dickinson's precision. I chose to form the sequence in mirror cinquains after reading Harryette Mullen's *Urban Tumbleweed: Notes from a Tanka Diary* (Graywolf Press, 2013); my thanks to Harryette.

"Field [1]"; "The Nothing"; and the initial draft of "Relentless" were written in a haunted hotel in Pipestone, MN on the anniversary of my mom's death. The only thing I read during that trip was Lara Mimosa Montes' *Thresholes* (Coffee House Press, 2020) and the poems are certainly influenced by that work; my thanks to Lara.

"Center" is informed by and partially built from these sources (my thanks to Karl for bearing his grief in public):

Boren, Cindy. "Karl-Anthony Towns says his 'soul has been killed off' by his mother's death from COVID." *The Washington Post*. December 24, 2020. Accessed online 3/20/21. https://www.washingtonpost.com/sports/2020/12/24/karl-anthony-towns-mother-covid/

Hine, Chris. "Karl-Anthony Towns' mother, Jacqueline Cruz-Towns, dies after COVID-19 battle." *The Star Tribune*. April 14, 2020. Accessed online 3/20/21. https://www.startribune.com/karl-anthony-towns-mother-jacqueline-cruz-dies-after-covid-19-battle/569602542/

Jordan, David K. "More about Obsidian." Accessed online 12/14/21. https://pages.ucsd.edu/~dkjordan/cgi-bin/moreabout.pl?tyimuh=obsidian

"Karl-Anthony Towns Postgame Press Conference - December 23, 2020." Accessed online 3/20/21. https://www.youtube.com/watch?v=qEgH03adz0A

"Obsidian." Accessed online 12/14/21. https://en.wikipedia.org/wiki/Obsidian

Towns, Karl-Anthony. THE TOUGHEST YEAR OF MY LIFE. Premiered November 2, 2020. Accessed online 3/20/21. https://www.youtube.com/watch?v=JEua1ilJ09U

[Image–grief wordmap]: these are scanned pages from my journal and these notes are from a workshop called "Genre Blenders" taught by Paula Cisewski in Spring 2021. The Kyle at the top of the page who says "lists are automatically lyrical" is Kyle Constalie.

"Relentless": An infinite, endlessly self-iterating version of this poem was published online by cloak.wtf; experience it here: https://c-l-o-a-k.itch.io/relentless. The epigraph quotes the therapist I saw directly following my mom's death. The lines concerning prayer reference a sermon India Johnson delivered at an Episcopal church in Iowa on Galentine's Day 2022, which I watched on the internet. India washes plague from textiles. Kelly Loija darns holes into wholeness. Hannah Chalew shovels bagasse and shreds plastic for paper fibers. "Relentless" is also influenced by The Creator card from Kim Krans' *Wild Unknown Archetypes* deck.

"The Nothing:" The words "May we all have the grit to openly drag the boat motors of our would-be rapists across their lawns and into our garages" directly quote or very closely paraphrase something my brother Christopher said, so 85% of that line is his. My only contribution is "tarnished in starlight like the nothing."

"Phantom Thread": The title and compass of the poem refer to Paul Thomas Anderson's 2017 film of the same name.

"Doubting Thomas": I looked at Caravaggio's painting *The Incredulity of Saint Thomas* (1601-1602) while drafting this poem.

"Field [3]": The phrase "everything is garbage," which was the poem's original title, is stolen from the character Captain Holt in season 3, episode 2 of *Brooklyn Nine-Nine*.

"We Can't Afford Horses": The title and first line are Amy Lorraine Long's, sent to me in an Instagram message. The next 4.5 lines are my response to Amy, which she recommended I put in a poem. Thank you, Amy.

"Heart Rate Cento": The sources of the cento's lines, in order of appearance, are as follows:

Robert Creeley "The Heart"; Sylvia Plath "Tulips"; William Shakespeare *King Lear*; George Oppen "Res Publica: 'The Poets Lie'"; James Baldwin "A Conversation with James Baldwin"; Eric Nelson–defense attorney in the trial of Derek Chauvin; Radiohead "No Surprises"; Kid Dakota "Age of Roaches"; C.D. Wright *One With Others*; Hanif Abdurraqib "Lights Out Tonight, Trouble in the Heartland"; Harryette Mullen *Urban Tumbleweed*; Reginald Dwayne Betts "Mural for the Heart"; At the Drive-In "Ebroglio"; Elliott Smith "Alameda"; Bessel van der Kolk *The Body Keeps the Score*; Sparklehorse "Heart of Darkness"; Blonde Redhead "Elephant Woman"; George Harrison, "Love Comes to Everyone"; Autolux "Anonymous"; Shannon Lay "Evil Eye"; Li Bai "Ch'Ang-Kan Village Song"; Christopher DeWeese "The Valley"; Zachary Schomburg "I Found Your Beating Heart Half-Buried"; Lenguas Largas "Yardsale Heart"; e.e. cummings "i carry your heart with me(i carry in my heart)"; Sun Yung Shin "명 부 젼 – 冥 府 殿 Myeongbujeon, the Hall of the Underworld"; The Knife "Heartbeats"; Tom Waits "Green Grass"; The Bible "Ezekiel 36:26"; Emily Dickinson "Heart, we will forget him"; Elizabeth Bishop "While Someone

Telephones"; Mazzy Star "Bells Ring."

My sincere thanks to these artists (with the exception of Eric Nelson; no thank you.)

"Field [4]" was written the day after I read *Ghost Guessed* by Paul Kwiatkowski and Tom Griggs (Presagio, 2018) on an airplane. My thanks to Paul and Tom.

Acknowledgements.

My sincere thanks to the editors of the following publications, where these poems first appeared, sometimes in alternate versions: 32 *Poems*: excerpts from "Ablation" "[River-]" and "[Treefall]"; *CLOAK*: "Relentless" (the *CLOAK* version is infinite, endlessly self-iterating: https://c-l-o-a-k.itch.io/relentless); *Concision*: "Field [2]"; *Harpy Hybrid Review*: "I mouth the word 'motherless'"; *Literary Mama*: excerpts from "Ablation" "[Covered]" and "[When I]"; *SELFFUCK*: "The Nothing"; *The Under Review*: "Center"; *Woodward Review*: "Heart Rate Cento"; and *Word for/ Word*: excerpts from "Ablation" "[A glacier moves through]"; "[See through the window]"; "[Atrium: open-roofed entrance]"; "[I want to show]"; [All my life fitted]"; and "[A glacier's weight]".

Thanks to my mom for my life; I hope your next one has been kinder. Thanks to my family, especially to my brothers Mike and Chris and my sister Amanda, with whom I survive, and to my dad for his love and for being solid ground. I realize some of the material in this book is personal and painful, and I hope you'll understand and forgive me for needing to reckon with its various and varying truths.

Thanks to Paula Cisewski, Joe Hall, and India Johnson for having eyes on the first draft of *Ablation* in two parts. Your thoughts on the poems and the community we share across space and time are world-deepening and priceless.

Thanks also to friends who read and shared their insights on individual pieces and/or the penultimate draft (sometimes over the phone in a disco nap room, sometimes in a restaurant that serves rice and beans, sometimes in the passenger seat of my car, sometimes on/in/over the internet): Logan Berry, Mike Corrao, Ethan Edwards, Angie Mazakis, Vincent Perrone, Tara Williams, and Morgan Grayce Willow. Your combined generosity constructed a safe place in which the book could grow, and I'm endlessly grateful.

Thanks to Michael Torres for feedback on "I mouth the word motherless…" that made it a better poem. This was the first poem from *Ablation* that I shared with another poet following my mom's death, and your care was immensely needed and appreciated. Thanks to Lucy LeMay, whose paintings and encouragement inspired what became the first draft of the title sequence "Ablation." Thanks to Jonathan Minton for publishing portions of an earlier draft of "Ablation" in Word for/Word and for consistently being one of the first editors to be open to the new + strange forms my work takes. Thanks to Meghan Maloney-Vinz at *The Under Review* for editorial suggestions for "Center" that helped me work it into its final form. Minds are better when they're not alone.

Deep and sincere thanks also to Hanif Abdurraqib, Elisa Gabbert, Matt Hart, Jenny Irish, Haley Lasché, Isaac Pickell, and Sun Yung Shin.

Thanks squared to Mike Corrao for bringing into being the infinite version of "Relentless" (and for suggesting aggressive fonts on a pink background), for his work laying out this monstrosity, and for designing the book's immaculate cover. Infinite light and gratitude to Andrew and Megan Wilt and everyone at 11:11 Press for your integrity and for believing in this book and allowing it to take the shape it needs.

Heartfelt thanks to these healers who offered their guidance at various points as these poems were written: Julie, Lura, and Cindy. You each aided my growth and healing in essential ways, and I thank you eternally and earnestly for your work and care.

I could watch exactly two things during the two months following my mom's death: Eric André's *Legalize Everything* (2020) and Nicole Byer's *Nailed It!* My thanks to Eric André and Nicole Byer for creating spaces for joy at a time when I had zero.